One

Clear

Call

First published in 2003

bradshaw books
Tigh Filí Arts Centre
Thompson House
MacCurtain Street
Cork, Ireland
Phone +353 21 4509274
Fax +353 21 4551617
e-mail bradshawbooks@cwpc.ie
Web www.tighfili.com

British Library Cataloguing in Publication Data
ISBN 0 949010 87 1

Cover art "Lolita and her Flea" by Jo Allen
reproduced by kind permission of Lesley Spillane, and Clare Bywater
Cover design, typeset and layout by Liz Willows
Printed and bound by Betaprint, Dublin

One Clear Call

a collection of poetry

by

Eugene O'Connell

bradshaw books
Cork

For Nora Bridget who saw us through

I have to please
The dead far longer than I need
To please the living; with them,
I have to live forever.

from *Antigone*
Sophocles

Acknowledgements

Acknowledgements are due to the editors of the following magazines and periodicals where some of these poems or versions of them have been published,
Poetry Ireland Review, The ShOp, A Sense of Cork 99, Southword, Poets Aloud Abú, Education Today (Journal of the Primary Teachers Association), The Yule Book, The Long Finger, Sliabh Luachra Magazine, Seanchas Duthalla, Another Room, The Steeple, Cork Review, Cork Literary Review, Poetry Scotland.

Eugene O'Connell has won Eacht Luachra and Munster Literature Centre *A Sense of Place* awards; he was one of the poets chosen by Ian Wild for his anthology *Poets for the Millennium.*

A selection of these poems can be heard on the CD (produced by Munster Literature Centre) to celebrate Cork Poetry in 2002,

The poem 'The Glass Purty' was broadcast on Lyric FM Radio.

The author gratefully acknowledges a grant award from Cork County Council (Arts Dept.) towards the publication of this book.

Special thanks to Liz Willows and Máire Bradshaw for their encouragement and editorial expertise.

Contents

Crossing The Fire

They never sat further apart
Than the space across the fire,
And even at the table – whose
Inside hugged the wall –
They sat at angles so that
If they wanted they could touch.
So when Johnie died we wanted
Nell to sit on his side of the fire,
Out of the way of the draught and
The traffic up to their room
But she kept to the habit
Of their life together and preferred,
The visitor to sit on his chair.
Afraid that if she crossed the fire
That there would be no one,
On the other side to return her gaze.

Dipper

for Mary Murphy

You wouldn't need an oar
To keep a Dipper under water,
Where he defies gravity to walk
As if it were the most
Natural thing in the world.
And maybe it's the world
We take for granted he wonders at,
When he surfaces to stand
On a stone in the street
That I was seeing for the first time,
Though we had walked it often
When your hand closed in mine.

Heron

It's the space around him
I envy, the poise of an acrobat,
How he need not move to paint
Different versions of himself
You can see from one bridge
And then other

                      where you find
Him reinvented, as a cast
A potter might have thrown,
Into a river that anchors him
On stilts so thin you could
Break them like matches.

Company

What was it he scoured the country for
On his morning trip to Williamstown?
A view of the rushy fields or the mountain
In the distance that appeared
At the whim of the weather,
Or something that dawned on him
When the company had gone,
And a door opened to let
The light flood in, and closed
On Denny Matty going in for his supper,
To leave him standing alone in the bar
And shiver at the evening drawing in.

The Virtue of Restraint

A master of the studied pause,
He would sup his tea and chew
Long before embarking on his yarn
And at the punch line exult in our cheer.
He preached the virtue of restraint
Imposed indeed a regimen of reserve,
So we held our noses at a sneeze,
Muffled our cups against a clink of spoon.

And so alerted to the need of his ways
We learned to read the signals at a whim
And could interpret the language of his mood,
If it blew hot or cold and only
His engine exiting the yard signalled,
The lifting of the curfew and we could
Exult like giddy yearlings in a paddock.

The Bargain

A tough man to make out, they said,
Would haggle till the last spit sealed his bargain.
There was the red stripper he bought that time,
Damaged goods that no kindness would placate,
And the spancel we lashed to her hindquarters
Was mere diversion as she flung ourselves
And the milking pail on to the weeping channel.
Then there was the cut price Kerry bought at auction
Who was reared in a dungeon without light
Bolting out the yard, two men swinging off her halter.

Though one time on the road he swerved
To let a rabbit escape his wheel and brought
The trembling creature home for our diversion.
So we set about concocting a flimsy hutch
Only to find the next day home school
The body hanging in the yard
Skinned and readied for the pot.
'How's a man to make out', he told our protest.

Skeeter

As ludicrous an invention as you could imagine
Bristling with teeth and steered by a wooden handle
You had to hoist to release the gathering swarthe.
Any stumble and you fell like the Roman on his spear
Your guts for garters in the meadow.

As it happened, that August, the weather broke
And we rushed to croher and point the crop
Into cocks to thwart the drizzle.
While my father hoisted the skeeter into the ditch
And promised to retrieve it but was distracted
By the Galway races and the meeting at Listowel.

So it settled there and seeded the first of it's winter coats
Till one morning I stumbled on it's russet rump
And pored like a scholar over an ancient icon
To interpret the subtext of it's flimsy frame...
And illuminate the promise he allowed to wither
And drift, pricklier than a rusted skeeter into age.

The Negev Desert

He would not resist
When we lugged him upstairs
To fall stocious on to the bed
Though one night his arm
Reached up and straightened
Like a grab, with his hand
Fully opened at the end
As if to face the sky
Like one of those giant dishes
That sit in the Negev desert
Watching and waiting for some signal
And when we looked to see
What we could make of the noises
That lodged in his throat
We saw that his eyes
Were not looking at us at all
But staring up at the ceiling and beyond

A Fool to Fortune

Oddly at home with the debris,
The remnant of his life around him,
He allowed pots to blacken and spill over,
The brush fully bristled to idle in the corner.

No longer a slave to time he would
Rise earlier to sup the first hailer of his day,
Carrying the title to his land in his coat
As he took to tout for bids in bars, a deed

That signalled the resolute nature of his intent.
Nor did the catheter faze him as they fixed
It's nozzle to his bladder, a mere accessory,
He jibed about his prowess now with the ladies.

Heedless to our concerns he rebuked our overture
And turned a deaf ear, the perfect defence
To allow him rail out of turn, flout the social graces,
Accepting what a fool to fortune he had become

And that the road that brought him to this place
Could not possibly have brought him to any other.

A Prayer to the Shoulder of the Cross

A practised eye he threw over the lumber
And selected the most amenable piece,
Steeled and weathered he could tell
To survive the rigour of his artifice.
At the workshop at home he would
Take the adze to plane its vulgar excesses
Hone it down to the bare essentials,
Let in the grooves to fit the cross-beam
And soak in oils to preserve its temper.

Strangely he never disposed of it for profit
Something counselled in him a need for its company
So that in his old age he would test the cross
Between his fingers, and shedding his inhibitions
Caress the rounded plane of its silky shoulder.

Likeness

Out for a drive I see
The sign of my father's hand
In the logo he mortared into
The end wall of the houses he built,
Modelled on the timber moulds
In the workshop at home.

What startles me though is how
My palms fold in his likeness
Over the wheel, my hands erect
And making a right angle,
His eyes looking at me the mirror.

Folly

The Folly at Roskeen I passed
Every day as a child had a reason,
Not like the Follies at the gates
Of the nearby estates in Castlemagner.
There was a door at the bottom
They would put a horse through,
To walk round and trample the grass
The men piked in from the top, so that
When the Silo filled up to the brim
The horse could walk out on to the bank.
But what if the weather broke – the question
That was always on my lips as I passed –
Or the men were called away,
Would the horse be condemned forever
To walk around his concrete tomb.

Spanish Smile

For a prank he had slashed
The laces at the lip of the leather
So that it smiled from ear to ear
And hung limp inside the Masters' coat.
Though it leaped erect at his anger,
To beat the hand of his errant pupil
And bathe in the juices he had secreted
Prophetically into his palm at lunch time.
Then returned to his pocket, to sit and smirk
At our do a cheathar, tri a cheathar
Carrying out the window and adding
Another note to the river song below,
Coiling out the Inches and on to the sea.

The Glass Purty

for Bernard O Donoghue

Say it was Lisleehane in the Glass Purty
When you shook it and not Lourdes
With the snow pouring on it's dreaming spires,
And you raced over fields for the cows
Instead of through an Alpine village,
Stopping for breath in the sharp air
To bathe your feet in the warm dung.
And Mary Anne was the only vision
To greet you on the journey home,
A shawled mannequin with a basket
On her way to the Egg Man with her hoard.

Taking It

When the barn fell
There was only air
To look into and imagine:
A space that was filled
Once each year with hay,
And steaming boys who came out
From the dark interior to cool themselves;
And retreated once the T.B.O
Had brought in its wynd and revved away,
Leaving Oul Mac to fill the silence
With his 'Is there anyone up there taking',
His great pikefulls that were banking
Off the lip of the shed,
Like Jumbos over Heathrow threatening
To fill up what was left of the sky.

Dalaigh

No matter what hour I turned in
I'd have to wind the clock for Dalaigh,
A neighbour up the road who lost
His fingers in the frost of Forty-Seven,
And only had a thumb in each hand
They had to mould a cup and saucer for.
Though he never told me, in the Sixties
When he traded the old clock for a new one
That it was powered by batteries and that
the wind-up key was a fake. So I still
Looked in at night and wound it for the morning
And only realised years on when he died and
Willed me the clock, that the hands could
Turn by themselves – and the gong still struck
On the hour to remind me that Dalaigh
Could have done the job without the fingers,
As far as the clock was concerned anyway.

A Charmer

for Jack Buckley

A charmer from the start
He won us with his yarns.
Like his antique tale of the servant boy
Strolling through Newmarket in the dawn,
A gust tugging at a housewife's hem
And as she raced to shield her modesty
He quipped 'Tis looking raw today ma'am'.

And then at dusk he would dance
A jig at the foot of the stairs,
A ploy though in his polished Wellingtons
To win my fathers attention and woo
His labouring wages for the day,
His passport to Martins' and the camaraderie
Of 'the blonde with the black skirt.'

And then one morning he was gone,
Only his body outline in the blanket
To confirm his presence once in our house.
He lost one leg we heard and then another
And appeared one night at the bar in wheels
And, seeing how lost we were for words,
Beckoned us to the table and the cards
And signalled the start of another yarn.
Though we knew the days of the polished Wellington
And the pounding of the 'Maids of Shinnagh'
At the foot of stairs were gone.

The Colour of Dereliction

The story of Denny Andy and his dog
Coloured our view of Araglen House,
As surely as the tinted sweet covers
We pulled across our eyes as children
Painted the world any shade we wanted ...

So we could never look at the gables
Of his house without imagining them
As the beak of a gearrchoc, stretched
To the limit for flies from a mother bird
Desperate to satisfy its craving.

Denny Andy himself would boast
Of the farm that went down his throat,
And how the dog he went to search for
In the pubs the morning after a session
Was a ruse to cadge a cure for his failing.

He was refused at Aggie's and he vowed
Never to darken the door of a pub again,
A promise he had time enough to savour
When his wife shocked the locality
By leaving him for someone sober.

The roof collapsed after he died,
But the legend lingered to stain
Our view of a house that would
Otherwise be bleached by the weather
Into the standard colour of dereliction.

Baubles

The Ri – buba of bi – yaaba, yaaba
Seated on his suganed throne
We peeled Bonhams from the litter
For his lusty blade to seam and flick
The baubles of their manhood
To Juno, our watchdog in the yard.
Oblivious to the old sows', hurish, hurish
He sprinkled the Dettol on the blushing gashes
And blessed the piglets screaming away
With his 'that'll stop ye're gallop for ye now'.

Delicate

Mere extra to the plot at the centre
Of old photographs, a tolerated aside,

He only ventured into the frame in high summer
And lived otherwise between fireplace and door,

A luxury to the needs of the bustling kitchen
They could ill afford though he carved

A niche in tending to the trivia about the hearth,
And in a bachelor household assumed a distaff role.

He lived long though and lingered into age
Needing less coaxing to stand in for the snap.

And found his true vocation in belted overcoat,
A gap-toothed parody to spoil their social graces.

Curlicue

Out of the corner of her eye, Maggie
Would see the curtains at Thade Michael's
Twitch when she passed with a bag of feed
On her back for the cows and was happy
When he sold the place and went to America
So she could do her jobs with dignity,
Realising years on when he came home
And stooped down to offer her his hand
The glint of recognition from their schooldays
When they laughed at the picture in the reader
Of the old monks lettering that had a face
At the end of a curlicue like an old woman's
That you had to stoop down and angle
Your head in line with the bench to look at.

Parog

An unlikely time traveller Parogs'
Once a week jaunt across the parish
to trade eggs for messages he carried
home on his shoulder to show people
He didn't want, came down through
Jule Bridgie who didn't want the memory
Worded in the good paper she kept sealed
In a press for special occasions, the ink
At the end of the refilled biro showing empty
When we scrambled to record the deed of
The glibly named cobbler, whose legendary
Outing had repercussions beyond the few wet
Steps he picked across a townland to shop.

Morley

Morley was blind and only left the house
On Sunday for mass and a drink afterwards
At Mrs Tims where he came alive with the porter
And clung to his wife all the way home.
Though he wondered after she died
If she was real at all or only a dream,
While he felt for the tea box and the ware
That she had stacked exactly for his fingers
To feel for so that he would not be thrown.

Tongues

'Ow Matt', was the first salute
Short for Matthew my Christian name
He'd taken up wrong the first day at school,
'Fuck you' a compliment above the noise
Of the bar when you attempted talk.
Bardolph to us sophisticates, flush with ale
His glowing face a beacon in the dark,
He drank whiskey off the floor once
A shard of broken glass catching a cavity
That festered for a week, sleeping overnight
another time at a function outside the parish
We thought he'd choke on his own snore,
The stops and starts in the night morse
For a languaged you'd need time to interpret,
A code that went with him, that no one broke.

Feral Child

His arms were locked at the elbow
And flapped in and out like wings
At our approach, so we had to
Make up a perch for him to roost
On the back of the Pick-Up tailed
Up to the door for his convenience,
He startled only once at the sound
Of someone taking a chisel to the Soaps
That blocked up the window of his loft,
And clucked at the noises coming out.

A kindly neighbour offered to build
An outside coop for the hens
We took out one by one in ours arms.
'To save the old couple the bother
Of wearing their knees on the stairs.'
He ventured to the company hurrying
To find the near way home before the dark.

Mapping the Interior

Imagine that you had a dishcloth
Bigger than the one mothers put on the bread
To slow its cooling, that you could spread
Over the whole kitchen floor to bring up its face
As clearly as the features on the cake.

You'd have a print you could lift up
To the light and examine for individual traces
Of people who came to swap yarns, and sit on
Sugan chairs that bit into the bare floor, leaving
Unique signatures on concrete that creased
Over time into a map you could look at and

Imagine what those amateur cartographers
Were thinking when their eyes fell, in the silence
Between the stories, that was broken only by
The sound of the fire and whatever it was that
Was calling in the night outside.

Buddha Ghiai

Buddha Ghiai in her last incarnation
Sitting near the fire, a rag in her fist
She smooths like a membrane over
A freshly baked cake she's imagined
To slow it's cooling, then stuffs the rag
Into her mouth before nodding off,
Slow to wrest it from her
We leave the comfort cloth
Between her teeth so she'll have
Something to taste when she wakes up.

Lane

Lane talked so much you'd
Think he had lost his calling
As a silver tongued charmer:
That the bone-setting was
Only a sideline; until you felt
His knee on your back and
The dull thud of bones moving
In places that distracted you
From the punch line of his story.

Jesus at Shea's

i.m. Jack Keeffe

Cheap-Jack for the country, Keeffe
Only stopped work as a gesture when
You drove into the yard and answered
'Craythur', to whatever character you
Brought up out of spite or otherwise
In the conversation, he gave out no
Commandment other than a caution
'To be than for the dry bed and the bite.'

                           You'd strain to hear
Him through the gaps in his mouth,
Wish he'd crop the big chest hair
That showed in the neckline of the
Two jumpers he wore against the cold,
But you knew who you had in the mirror
As you drove out of the yard and what
He'd say to your wish for Shea, the boss
Who'd have him out in any weather.

The Sixty-Four Man

for Con O'Connor

Connors never went to the village
After that championship season,
Never saw the anniversary photo
In the local pub that had the legend
'Our Silver heroes where have they gone'

His colours became the red of Meelin;
The grey of Doneraile stone he dressed,
Until the heap of flags he'd cut to grace
The front of other peoples houses dwarfed
The mound of rock brought in that morning.

His finger had thickened to mock
The delicate hands that would pluck
A ball out of the air in Sixty-Four,
And stiffened so that he had to peel
Them away from the handle of the hammer.

And the odd time he lifted his eyes
To scan the parish he saw his own
Generation thin, the memories of his deeds
Recede like the rough edges of the stone
He chipped at until the grain showed.

Letters from Africa

I had to stack the letters
Against a briar, like the folds
Of a melodeon, that I pulled
Towards me to make a draught,
To redden the envelopes that
Were so fine when you posted them
I had to cut them with a blade,
In case I'd have to stitch any word
That I had missed with Sellotape.
Now the red white and blue edges
Of your letters from Africa are burning
In my backyard, and no matter
How much I prime the bellows
Of my makeshift melodeon
I can't knock a tune out of it.

Open Plan

It appears that Dolphin enjoy
Resting their heads on a pillar of
Seaweed when they sleep

Your armchair had no rest
For your back to lean into,
Or no pillow under you to fluff.
Though your drink was near
And you had no need
To go into kitchen for a coffee,
And the room you stepped into
Was three dimensional and deepened,
To included all those strangers
Who bothered you, and you wondered
How you mislaid the stairway
That would have taken you to sleep.

Dramatic Gesture

Standing on Nano Nagle Bridge
I thought of Kate Winslett on the prow
Of the *Titanic* and was tempted to
Step on to the rail and lift my hands
Up to the sky in a dramatic gesture,
Except that the bundle of shopping under
My arm and the case with the organiser
Would fall into the water and be carried
Out of the city, and there would be
No one at my back to break the fall
If a gust decided to blow up the Lee.

Miltown Mardi Gras

The squalls would drive you into the bars
At Miltown Malbay where you'd stand
Near the 'session' pretending an interest
In the music when you read the lettering
On the back of sweating men, the stain
Seeping out of Blind Boys towards Alabama
Making you wonder if they had as many shirt
Changes in their repertoire as tunes, that moved
You to sway with the Crusties and their women,
Answering Yeah Man and forgetting that
You were 'forty and looking' while
The world and his wife bawled their pleasure
Into the streets at Miltown Mardi Gras.

Testing the Water

Say I'd crossed from Passage East
To Ballyhack in a mythical hay float,
Pulled by a horse who bolted when
I fell off the sloped end into the sea.
And didn't stop until he reached
Your yard at Bannow, would you
Leap onto his back and race
Out into the Sound, cup my life blood
The coloured froth in your hands and drink
Saying words out of your red lips.

The Spirit Bowl

When you go to the city
To break it off with your lover
Make sure he is not a glassblower
Who would put his mouth to yours
Blow into the pipe of your throat
a spirit bowl that would glow
Inside of you when you thought of him.

The Pleasure Giver

Shrivelled up like an old prune,
There are women who stand at bus stops
Catching one hand in the other and waiting
On the hinge of expectancy for some door
To open, thumbing beads that have faded
To the colour of their clothes, buttoned
At the neck for fear of giving pleasure,
They reserve for an imagined god
Stripped to his underclothes and hanging
Above them in a pose that would have
A younger woman in floods, in a place
You could only tell from the stare in her eye
And the heightened colour of her cheek.

Dannox

For diversion Dannox would
Go to the city once a week
Change into his dancing clothes
And put a tape into the recorder.

He'd tiptoe round the traps of his trade
Laid out on the street in front of him
On hob nailed shoes that sounded
On the gleaming pavement flags.

But he was in his element once he pressed
The button and the music started, pushing
Out his brace with his thumbs and gesturing
At the people who looked at him.

Mouthing the words of the song on the recorder
'Waiting for you to say you love me, say you love me'
And leaping into the air like a puppet, on strings
You looked hard to see but couldn't.

Ryesha

There was no sex in Ireland
Before the *Late Late Show*
They tell us, though "Ryesha"
The Irish word for 'sweat of lovers'
Survived in the workaday banter
Of the women of my youth as code
For what was good and wholesome,
So it was "Ryesha" this and "Ryesha" that
Until the day closed and couples peeled
Their standard issue aprons and Wellingtons
Away before kneeling for the rosary,
And retiring to continue the joyful mysteries
In the room above, discarding the beads
On the shoulder of a chair, a makeshift
Geiger counter that trembled at first to register
The ruckus and then slowed to a dead plumb.

The Realisation

To hear that Cuckoo again, does
It mean more than the realisation
That shook you into recall,
Of how some ancestor of his
Must have boomed his note
Out of that same wood
And stopped your labour that day,
So that you rose with the company
To ease the ache in your back,
And trace between smokes the history
Of the Jones' in these parts,
Before you bent again to hear the Slean
Slicing through the bog and never thought,
That next time your visitor would sing
Out of these woods to you alone.

The Bow Crow

The Bow Crow, an Bhanbh Chath – the earth goddess, was said to hang over the battlefield and feed on the remains of the dead

Jones took one step to our two,
Only stopping to read the track
Of something that passed in the night,
Teaching us to interpret the sign.

So when we stopped at his place
Years on it was the call of a crow
That made us look up for a signal,
Rather than done among the rubble.

Mimicking his posture in the bar,
Aloof from the company, head angled
On his neck and fixed on the distance,
While the froth settled in his glass.

The Letter

for D.J.C

He left no written account on his life
So we had to fill out the details
From bits and scraps: initials
He inscribed on some job or odd
Insignia like the Star of David
He painted high up in a barn:
And the pages of a letter that survived
His first trip to London and surfaced
Years on in my hand, inquiring
After the company at home – telling
Of his prospects and how he got
The start from some local legend
He ran into in Kilburn –
Before breaking off with observations
About the weather on the flight out
'The sun was shining and there was
A film of cloud under us ' But
'When we went under the clouds it rained'.

Dead Man Walking

He would race the Corsair
Up the Rock Road until
The front wheel broke through the floor
And lifted his passenger into the roof;
And bite his glass in the bar
To work the silvers over his tongue,
As prelude to his joust with Thady
When they closed with knives,
Though we knew when the tumour
Swelled inside his head and
He took to wearing soft-soled shoes
That he had done with tempting fate.

Reluctant Passengers

The needle touching thirty
The Corsair took to wobble
A shiver at the start that
Later sent the body into spasm.
And left it sprawling helpless on the road
Though Daniel would race to clutch the steering,
Steady the nerves of us reluctant passengers.

Once at the Quarry Cross
We went full circle and carved
A neat rubber ellipse on the road
And spilled Jack Hickey out swearing
To retrace his footsteps to the Shamrocks
And how 'he'd never travel with us again'.

Perhaps it was that touching thirty
He sensed his life expectancy was slipping
Or that he baulked at the ominous spasm
In this left arm that urged attention
And he took to eyeball things a bit,
Live on the edge and leave us reluctant passengers
Scrambling to collect our senses
To fill the vacant gaps at our leisure
The bigger picture of his absence after.

The Mockea Bird

Years on I had to move
Forward and back to focus
On the mockea bird
Who lost his footing when
The spring he stood on collapsed.

So that his tail hung out
Through the bars of the cage
Danny Joe bought at some outing
And tacked on to the ceiling
To be sounded by the draught.

And stop myself from pushing
At the cymbals that hardly sounded
Now through the rust, afraid
That the keepsake would fall
To join the mouse's fossil on the floor.

Omens

Cows always take the easiest path
Dead level to suit their ambling shuffle
Which was why the builders of the first
American roads took the ancient buffalo routes.
Foxes are different though, they blaze
A vertical trail over ditches,
Scatter decoys in your wake to spoil the chase.

Badgers are erratic, will disperse wodges of earth
Any old how and leave no directive
To chart the route to their winter burrow.
Above though, the November flocks impress
Carve a V and tell you exactly where they are headed.

So why should I still look out for omens
When I can track to a T the path my brother
Took across these fields before he left us,
And worry about what signposts I can turn to
To chart my progress when I've exhausted
All the pathways of earth and sky.

Pingoes

Not more than two fields away
The rounded barrow of a fossil Pingo,
Though no one bothered to alert me to
The earthly bank of its charmed circle.

Too taken with farm chores
Pitting potatoes or thinning mangolds,
And Sunday the spare day
Was for lofting bowls or flaking leather.

So it was late in life I stumbled into
The fossil Pingo of the beaker people,
The round barrow that Paddy Flor
Dreading the fairies had meticulously preserved.

And now that the barns have rusted
And the yard has shed its pious elders,
The Pingo thrives and everywhere proclaims
The enchanted country I discovered late.

And was only the next townland
Not two fields away, a stones throw
And yet the distance between earth and sky
The fossil Pingoes of the Meeing.

A Habit

Someone had thrown out the cross
That stood in the middle of the enclosure
At Gougane Barra, and had a teak
Copy put in its place. The people
Still stuck pennies into the old cross
So it grew a copper skin that stood
After the wood had rotted. The habit
Trickled on to nearby branches that
Were punctured as far as they could reach
With whatever coin they had to hand,
And visitors coming to photograph the
Object of devotion wondered at people who
Put their money into such a practise.

Touched

You were leisurely that day
And broke the remainder
Of your bread to fling at sparrows
That foraged among the weld
And shavings of your forge,
And might have landed in the palm
Of your hand if you stretched it out
And nested there so you'd become
The talk of the place
Your hammers rested on the bench
And no one to stoke the embers
Of your fire dying in the corner.

The Mower

In the heat of the day he would
Open out the doors of his tractor
So that they would beat in and out
Like wings, to cool him while
He circled the meadow that receded
To the one last swathe he cut with relish,
Before setting the mower for the road home.

Though in his old age the neighbours
Would complain him for taking the road
For a meadow and opening out the doors,
So that he looked like he was riding
Some great blue bird that beat its wings
To lift into flight, while the cars stalled
In his wake and drivers blared their horns.

Groundwork

He never trucked with Mystics
Or the like, and he would no more
Have wanted us to compare him to
The rich young man of the Gospels
Than the man in the moon,
Though he did walk out of his house
Leaving the doors open and the radio blaring,
So we could see after he died that
All his earthly goods were rusted,
That he must have treasure in Heaven,

Though the sign of his hand around the place
Would point us down for his salvation
To the earth that he worked all his life
And dug to hold his neighbours,
Who seemed content in the plot
The parish had set aside for them

The Undertakers Art

He had slipped away from her
Long before he died, so Sheila
Had to think hard to arrive at
An expression she could lay him out in
So she settled for a standard
'Ready to break into a smile',
So he'd be presentable for the neighbours
Who remembered that, whatever else about him,
He was the first to return the Coher.
So they talked in his favour and vied
Over who had seen him last
On Pleasure Hill, before he walked
Off the road and into the dark.

Hansel

Like Hansel in the story
He had left a trail of crumbs

To lead him home: but the birds
Came in the night so he had no way back,
And since he was old now, his father
The woodcutter and stepmother were gone
And Gretel was taken up with her own care,
He lost his appetite for witches and
Pots of gold at the end of the rainbow;
So he decided to bed down where he was
Leaving his cap, pants and boots scattered
Along the Inches, a pebbled trail
To start the story for them,
When they found him in the river.